Energy flows where focus goes.

SAM PENNY
The Topify Method

topifymethod.com

Chips Investments Pty Ltd
Parcel Collect 10042 76215
Shop 4, 44 Landsborough Parade
Golden Beach QLD 4551 Australia

Chips
Investments
AUST

Chips Investments Pty Ltd is the publisher of this book. More information can be found at www.topifymethod.com.

Copyright © Sam Penny 2025

All rights reserved. No part of this book may be reproduced, stored in a retrieval system, or transmitted in any form or by any means—electronic, mechanical, photocopying, recording, or otherwise—without prior written permission from the publisher, except for brief quotations used in a review or critical analysis.

A CIP catalogue record for this book is available from the National Library of Australia.
ISBN 978-1-7638968-0-2

Design by Sam Penny

Chips Investments Pty Ltd is committed to sustainability. This book is printed on paper sourced from responsibly managed forests.

DEDICATION

To all those who want to achieve more with their life.

How to Use The Topify Method

Welcome to The Topify Method, your simple and effective tool for staying focused and making progress every day. This journal is designed for everyone—mums, business owners, travellers, artists—anyone looking to make the most of their time and achieve more.

At the heart of this planner is The Topify Method—a simple yet powerful system to help you align your daily actions with your bigger goals. Each Quarter, Month, Week, and Day, you'll write down your Top 5 priorities and focus on completing at least the Top 1. Small steps, taken consistently, lead to big results.

Celebrate each achievement!

SCAN TO
LEARN
MORE

How to Achieve More

Quarterly Focus
Write down your Top 3 Priorities for the next three months. These will guide your monthly and weekly plans to ensure every step moves you forward.

Monthly Focus
From your quarterly goals, choose the Top 5 things to accomplish this month. Keep it clear and actionable.

Weekly Focus
Break your monthly goals into smaller actions. Write down the Top 5 tasks for the week and focus on making progress.

Daily Focus
Each day, list your Top 5 tasks and commit to completing at least the Top 1. Progress comes from action.

Reflection & Looking Ahead
Take a moment at the end of each period—whether it's a day, week, month, or quarter—to reflect on your progress. What worked well? What challenges did you overcome? Celebrate your achievements, no matter how small. Then, look ahead—what's the next step to keep moving forward?

This planner is here to simplify your productivity, keep you focused, and help you achieve more—one step at a time. Let's make every day count!

SCAN TO LEARN MORE

Quarter: _____ to _____

My 3 Big Priorities This Quarter

Priority 1:

_____
_____

Priority 2:

_____
_____

Priority 3:

_____
_____

Why these 3?

Priority 1:

_____
_____

Priority 2:

_____
_____

Priority 3:

_____
_____

What Does Success Look Like?

Priority 1: _____

_____

Priority 2: _____

_____

Priority 3: _____

_____

My Top 5 for Alignment

Main Focus: _____

Consistent Action: _____

Quick Wins: _____

_____

_____

Biggest Challenge: _____

One Rule to Follow: _____

Quarterly Commitment Statement

I commit to _____ over the next 90 days because _____

_____

_____

Month: _____

My Top 5 for this Month

Top 1 Done

○ ☐ _____

○ ☐ _____

○ ☐ _____

○ ☐ _____

○ ☐ _____

Are these aligned with my Quarterly Top 5?

Energy flows, where focus goes.

Week Starting: _____

(2)

My Top 5 for this Week

Top 1   Done

○ ☐ _____

○ ☐ _____

○ ☐ _____

○ ☐ _____

○ ☐ _____

Are these aligned with my Monthly Top 5?

Your future self is watching - go!

My top 5 for today

Top 1 Done

○ ☐ _____

○ ☐ _____

○ ☐ _____

○ ☐ _____

○ ☐ _____

Are these aligned with my Weekly Top 5?

Progress beats perfection—take one step forward today, no matter how small.

Date: _____ Day: _____   (1)

My top win today was: _____

Today I am grateful for: _____

My top 5 for today

Top 1   Done

○ ☐ _____

○ ☐ _____

○ ☐ _____

○ ☐ _____

○ ☐ _____

Are these aligned with my Weekly Top 5?

A brighter tomorrow is a consequence of a purposeful today.

Date: _____ Day: _____ (2)

My top win today was: _____

Today I am grateful for: _____

My top 5 for today

Top 1 Done

○ ☐ _____

○ ☐ _____

○ ☐ _____

○ ☐ _____

○ ☐ _____

Are these aligned with my Weekly Top 5?

Make yourself proud by staying on track.

Date: _____   Day: _____   (3)

_____
_____
_____
_____
_____
_____
_____
_____
_____
_____
_____
_____
_____
_____
_____
_____
_____
_____
_____
_____
_____
_____
_____

My top win today was: _____

Today I am grateful for: _____

My top 5 for today

Top 1 Done

○ ☐ _____

○ ☐ _____

○ ☐ _____

○ ☐ _____

○ ☐ _____

Are these aligned with my Weekly Top 5?

Goals exist to be met, not just imagined
—get moving.

Date: _____ Day: _____ ④

My top win today was:

Today I am grateful for:

My top 5 for today

Top 1 Done

○ ☐ _____

○ ☐ _____

○ ☐ _____

○ ☐ _____

○ ☐ _____

Are these aligned with my Weekly Top 5?

Rise above your fears by believing in your worth.

Date: _____ Day: _____ (5)

My top win today was:

Today I am grateful for:

My top 5 for today

Top 1   Done

○ ☐ _____

○ ☐ _____

○ ☐ _____

○ ☐ _____

○ ☐ _____

Are these aligned with my Weekly Top 5?

Live for you, because ultimately you're the one facing your own reflection.

Date: _____ Day: _____ ⑥

My top win today was:

Today I am grateful for:

My top 5 for today

Top 1   Done

○ ☐ _____

○ ☐ _____

○ ☐ _____

○ ☐ _____

○ ☐ _____

Are these aligned with my Weekly Top 5?

When focus leads, success always follows.

Date: _____ Day: _____   (7)

My top win today was:

Today I am grateful for:

Week Ending: _____

(1)

My Week in Review

My top win this week was:

I am grateful for:

What could be improved or learned:

Week Starting: _____

My Top 5 for this Week

Top 1   Done

○ ☐ _____

○ ☐ _____

○ ☐ _____

○ ☐ _____

○ ☐ _____

Are these aligned with my Monthly Top 5?

Done is better than perfect.

My top 5 for today

Top 1　Done

○ ☐ _____

○ ☐ _____

○ ☐ _____

○ ☐ _____

○ ☐ _____

Are these aligned with my Weekly Top 5?

Rise up, show up, and finish what you start.

Date: _____   Day: _____   (8)

_____
_____
_____
_____
_____
_____
_____
_____
_____
_____
_____
_____
_____
_____
_____
_____
_____
_____
_____
_____
_____
_____
_____

My top win today was: _____

Today I am grateful for: _____

My top 5 for today

Top 1   Done

◯ ☐ _____

◯ ☐ _____

◯ ☐ _____

◯ ☐ _____

◯ ☐ _____

Are these aligned with my Weekly Top 5?

You're allowed to be your biggest fan—
believe in yourself when no one else will.

Date: _____ Day: _____ (9)

My top win today was:

Today I am grateful for:

My top 5 for today

Top 1 Done

○ ☐ _____

○ ☐ _____

○ ☐ _____

○ ☐ _____

○ ☐ _____

Are these aligned with my Weekly Top 5?

Grateful thoughts lead to kind actions
and a life well-lived.

Date: _____ Day: _____   (10)

My top win today was: _____

Today I am grateful for: _____

My top 5 for today

Top 1 Done

○ ☐ _____

○ ☐ _____

○ ☐ _____

○ ☐ _____

○ ☐ _____

Are these aligned with my Weekly Top 5?

Anchor yourself in the here and now, so your dreams have room to grow.

Date: _____ Day: _____   (11)

My top win today was: _____

Today I am grateful for: _____

My top 5 for today

Top 1 Done

○ ☐ _____

○ ☐ _____

○ ☐ _____

○ ☐ _____

○ ☐ _____

Are these aligned with my Weekly Top 5?

Chase actions, not illusions.

Date: _____ Day: _____ (12)

My top win today was: _____

Today I am grateful for: _____

My top 5 for today

Top 1   Done

○ ☐ _____

○ ☐ _____

○ ☐ _____

○ ☐ _____

○ ☐ _____

Are these aligned with my Weekly Top 5?

Savour the day you have, so the days ahead unfold with clarity.

Date: _____ Day: _____ (13)

My top win today was: _____

Today I am grateful for: _____

My top 5 for today

Top 1 Done

○ ☐ _____

○ ☐ _____

○ ☐ _____

○ ☐ _____

○ ☐ _____

Are these aligned with my Weekly Top 5?

Their dismissal is proof you must value
yourself more fiercely.

Date: _____   Day: _____   (14)

_____
_____
_____
_____
_____
_____
_____
_____
_____
_____
_____
_____
_____
_____
_____
_____
_____
_____
_____
_____
_____
_____
_____
_____

My top win today was: _____
_____

Today I am grateful for: _____
_____

Week Ending: _____

My Week in Review

My top win this week was:

I am grateful for:

What could be improved or learned:

Week Starting: _____

My Top 5 for this Week

Top 1   Done
○ □ _____

○ □ _____

○ □ _____

○ □ _____

○ □ _____

Are these aligned with my Monthly Top 5?

Small steps, big results.

My top 5 for today

Top 1   Done

○ ☐ _____

○ ☐ _____

○ ☐ _____

○ ☐ _____

○ ☐ _____

Are these aligned with my Weekly Top 5?

Their dismissal is proof you must value yourself more fiercely.

Date: _____ Day: _____ (15)

_____
_____
_____
_____
_____
_____
_____
_____
_____
_____
_____
_____
_____
_____
_____
_____
_____
_____
_____
_____
_____
_____
_____

My top win today was: _____

Today I am grateful for: _____

My top 5 for today

Top 1 Done

○ ☐ _____

○ ☐ _____

○ ☐ _____

○ ☐ _____

○ ☐ _____

Are these aligned with my Weekly Top 5?

While perfection stands still, progress takes the next step.

Date: _____ Day: _____ (16)

My top win today was:

Today I am grateful for:

My top 5 for today

Top 1   Done

○ ☐ _____

○ ☐ _____

○ ☐ _____

○ ☐ _____

○ ☐ _____

Are these aligned with my Weekly Top 5?

Savour the now, because within it lies
the seed of all that's to come.

Date: _____ Day: _____ (17)

My top win today was: _____

Today I am grateful for: _____

My top 5 for today

Top 1 Done

○ ☐ _____

○ ☐ _____

○ ☐ _____

○ ☐ _____

○ ☐ _____

Are these aligned with my Weekly Top 5?

Deep focus trumps shallow busyness every single day.

Date: _____ Day: _____ (18)

My top win today was:

Today I am grateful for:

My top 5 for today

Top 1   Done

○ ☐ _____

○ ☐ _____

○ ☐ _____

○ ☐ _____

○ ☐ _____

Are these aligned with my Weekly Top 5?

When you nurture the core of what matters, distractions melt away.

Date: _____ Day: _____   (19)

My top win today was: _____

Today I am grateful for: _____

My top 5 for today

Top 1 Done

○ ☐ _____

○ ☐ _____

○ ☐ _____

○ ☐ _____

○ ☐ _____

Are these aligned with my Weekly Top 5?

See challenges as chances—gratitude converts them into growth.

Date: _____ Day: _____ (20)

My top win today was: _____

Today I am grateful for: _____

My top 5 for today

Top 1 Done

○ ☐ _____

○ ☐ _____

○ ☐ _____

○ ☐ _____

○ ☐ _____

Are these aligned with my Weekly Top 5?

Let their silence fuel your drive to prove yourself to yourself.

Date: _____ Day: _____ (21)

My top win today was: _____

Today I am grateful for: _____

Week Ending: _____ (3)

My Week in Review

My top win this week was:

_____
_____
_____

I am grateful for:

_____
_____
_____

What could be improved or learned:

_____
_____

Week Starting: _____

My Top 5 for this Week

Top 1 Done

○ ☐ _____

○ ☐ _____

○ ☐ _____

○ ☐ _____

○ ☐ _____

Are these aligned with my Monthly Top 5?

One task. Full focus. Crush it.

My top 5 for today

Top 1 Done

○ ☐ _____

○ ☐ _____

○ ☐ _____

○ ☐ _____

○ ☐ _____

Are these aligned with my Weekly Top 5?

Champions aren't crowned in bed—rise and grind.

Date: _____   Day: _____   (22)

My top win today was: _____

Today I am grateful for: _____

My top 5 for today

Top 1 Done
○ ☐ _____

○ ☐ _____

○ ☐ _____

○ ☐ _____

○ ☐ _____

Are these aligned with my Weekly Top 5?

See the good in who you are right now.

Date: _____ Day: _____   (23)

My top win today was: _____

Today I am grateful for: _____

My top 5 for today

Top 1 Done

○ ☐ _____

○ ☐ _____

○ ☐ _____

○ ☐ _____

○ ☐ _____

Are these aligned with my Weekly Top 5?

Devote yourself to the here and now—
only then can your future bloom.

Date: _____ Day: _____ (24)

My top win today was: _____

Today I am grateful for: _____

My top 5 for today

Top 1   Done

○ ☐ _____

○ ☐ _____

○ ☐ _____

○ ☐ _____

○ ☐ _____

Are these aligned with my Weekly Top 5?

Busy is an illusion; real work is tangible progress.

Date: _____ Day: _____ (25)

My top win today was: _____

Today I am grateful for: _____

My top 5 for today

Top 1 Done

○ ☐ _____

○ ☐ _____

○ ☐ _____

○ ☐ _____

○ ☐ _____

Are these aligned with my Weekly Top 5?

Seeing the good in life starts with a grateful perspective.

Date: _____ Day: _____ (26)

_____
_____
_____
_____
_____
_____
_____
_____
_____
_____
_____
_____
_____
_____
_____
_____
_____
_____
_____
_____
_____
_____
_____
_____

My top win today was: _____

Today I am grateful for: _____

My top 5 for today

Top 1   Done

○ ☐ _____

○ ☐ _____

○ ☐ _____

○ ☐ _____

○ ☐ _____

Are these aligned with my Weekly Top 5?

Make your present a masterpiece, and
your future will be your legacy.

Date: _____ Day: _____ (27)

My top win today was: _____

Today I am grateful for: _____

My top 5 for today

Top 1 Done

○ ☐ _____

○ ☐ _____

○ ☐ _____

○ ☐ _____

○ ☐ _____

Are these aligned with my Weekly Top 5?

Choose discipline over distraction to build the life you envision.

Date: _____ Day: _____ (28)

My top win today was: _____

Today I am grateful for: _____

Week Ending: _____

My Week in Review

My top win this week was:
_____
_____
_____

I am grateful for:
_____
_____
_____

What could be improved or learned:
_____
_____

Week Starting: _____

My Top 5 for this Week

Top 1 Done

○ ☐ _____

○ ☐ _____

○ ☐ _____

○ ☐ _____

○ ☐ _____

Are these aligned with my Monthly Top 5?

Win the day, every day.

My top 5 for today

Top 1 Done

○ ☐ _____

○ ☐ _____

○ ☐ _____

○ ☐ _____

○ ☐ _____

Are these aligned with my Weekly Top 5?

Respect your craft by respecting your time.

Date: _____ Day: _____ (29)

My top win today was: _____

Today I am grateful for: _____

My top 5 for today

Top 1 Done

○ ☐ _____

○ ☐ _____

○ ☐ _____

○ ☐ _____

○ ☐ _____

Are these aligned with my Weekly Top 5?

Find reasons to be grateful now, and the future opens its doors wider.

Date: _____ Day: _____ (30)

My top win today was: _____

Today I am grateful for: _____

My top 5 for today

Top 1 Done
○ ☐ _____

○ ☐ _____

○ ☐ _____

○ ☐ _____

○ ☐ _____

Are these aligned with my Weekly Top 5?

Goals need legs—let your daily tasks be their strides.

Date: _____ Day: _____ (31)

My top win today was: _____

Today I am grateful for: _____

Month: _____

My Month in Review

My top win last month was:

_____
_____

I am grateful for:

_____
_____

What could be improved or learned:

_____
_____

Month: _____

My Top 5 for this Month

Top 1 Done
○ ☐ _____

○ ☐ _____

○ ☐ _____

○ ☐ _____

○ ☐ _____

Are these aligned with my Quarterly Top 5?

Less thinking, more doing.

Week Ending: _____

My Week in Review

My top win this week was:

_____
_____
_____

I am grateful for:

_____
_____
_____

What could be improved or learned:

_____
_____

Week Starting: _____

My Top 5 for this Week

Top 1 Done

○ ☐ _____

○ ☐ _____

○ ☐ _____

○ ☐ _____

○ ☐ _____

Are these aligned with my Monthly Top 5?

Success loves speed.

My top 5 for today

Top 1   Done
○ ☐ _____

○ ☐ _____

○ ☐ _____

○ ☐ _____

○ ☐ _____

Are these aligned with my Weekly Top 5?

Seize the morning, and you'll own the night.

Date: _____ Day: _____ (1)

My top win today was: _____

Today I am grateful for: _____

My top 5 for today

Top 1   Done

○ ☐ _____

○ ☐ _____

○ ☐ _____

○ ☐ _____

○ ☐ _____

Are these aligned with my Weekly Top 5?

Stop waiting for praise—use self-respect as your loudest cheerleader.

Date: _____ Day: _____ ②

_____
_____
_____
_____
_____
_____
_____
_____
_____
_____
_____
_____
_____
_____
_____
_____
_____
_____
_____
_____
_____
_____
_____
_____

My top win today was: _____

Today I am grateful for: _____

My top 5 for today

Top 1   Done

○ ☐ _____

○ ☐ _____

○ ☐ _____

○ ☐ _____

○ ☐ _____

Are these aligned with my Weekly Top 5?

When perfection tries to steal your moment, remember: progress is the real prize.

Date: _____ Day: _____ (3)

My top win today was: _____

Today I am grateful for: _____

My top 5 for today

Top 1 Done

○ ☐ _____

○ ☐ _____

○ ☐ _____

○ ☐ _____

○ ☐ _____

Are these aligned with my Weekly Top 5?

Set fire to your day—burn through every obstacle.

Date: _____ Day: _____ (4)

My top win today was: _____

Today I am grateful for: _____

My top 5 for today

Top 1 Done

○ ☐ _____

○ ☐ _____

○ ☐ _____

○ ☐ _____

○ ☐ _____

Are these aligned with my Weekly Top 5?

Find peace in your present, and your future will shine brighter.

Date: _____ Day: _____ ⑤

My top win today was: _____

Today I am grateful for: _____

My top 5 for today

Top 1   Done

○ ☐ _____

○ ☐ _____

○ ☐ _____

○ ☐ _____

○ ☐ _____

Are these aligned with my Weekly Top 5?

Channel time into tasks that inch you closer to success.

Date: _____   Day: _____   (6)

My top win today was: _____

Today I am grateful for: _____

My top 5 for today

Top 1   Done
○ □ _____

○ □ _____

○ □ _____

○ □ _____

○ □ _____

Are these aligned with my Weekly Top 5?

Set the pace, and your productivity will soar.

Date: _____   Day: _____   (7)

My top win today was: _____

Today I am grateful for: _____

Week Ending: _____ (6)

My Week in Review

My top win this week was:

_____
_____

I am grateful for:

_____
_____

What could be improved or learned:

_____
_____

Week Starting: _____

My Top 5 for this Week

Top 1 Done

○ ☐ _____

○ ☐ _____

○ ☐ _____

○ ☐ _____

○ ☐ _____

Are these aligned with my Monthly Top 5?

Action beats intention - start now, refine later.

My top 5 for today

Top 1 Done

○ ☐ _____

○ ☐ _____

○ ☐ _____

○ ☐ _____

○ ☐ _____

Are these aligned with my Weekly Top 5?

Be brave enough to dream a little bigger for yourself.

Date: _____ Day: _____   (8)

_____
_____
_____
_____
_____
_____
_____
_____
_____
_____
_____
_____
_____
_____
_____
_____
_____
_____
_____
_____
_____
_____
_____
_____

My top win today was: _____

Today I am grateful for: _____

My top 5 for today

Top 1   Done

○ ☐ _____

○ ☐ _____

○ ☐ _____

○ ☐ _____

○ ☐ _____

Are these aligned with my Weekly Top 5?

When perfection holds you back, let progress lead you forward.

Date: _____ Day: _____ ⑨

My top win today was:

Today I am grateful for:

My top 5 for today

Top 1 Done

○ ☐ _____

○ ☐ _____

○ ☐ _____

○ ☐ _____

○ ☐ _____

Are these aligned with my Weekly Top 5?

Set your priorities by what resonates with your heart, not by what's urgent.

Date: _____ Day: _____ (10)

My top win today was: _____

Today I am grateful for: _____

My top 5 for today

Top 1 Done

○ ☐ _____

○ ☐ _____

○ ☐ _____

○ ☐ _____

○ ☐ _____

Are these aligned with my Weekly Top 5?

Be here fully; your future will thank you
for this unwavering focus.

Date: _____ Day: _____ (11)

My top win today was: _____

Today I am grateful for: _____

My top 5 for today

Top 1 Done

○ ☐ _____

○ ☐ _____

○ ☐ _____

○ ☐ _____

○ ☐ _____

Are these aligned with my Weekly Top 5?

Chase your goals like they owe you money.

Date: _____ Day: _____ (12)

My top win today was:

Today I am grateful for:

My top 5 for today

Top 1   Done
○ ☐ _____

○ ☐ _____

○ ☐ _____

○ ☐ _____

○ ☐ _____

Are these aligned with my Weekly Top 5?

Shine fearlessly because the world needs your light.

Date: _____   Day: _____   (13)

My top win today was: _____

Today I am grateful for: _____

My top 5 for today

Top 1 Done

○ ☐ _____

○ ☐ _____

○ ☐ _____

○ ☐ _____

○ ☐ _____

Are these aligned with my Weekly Top 5?

Gratitude is a choice; make it daily and watch your outlook change.

Date: _____   Day: _____   (14)

My top win today was:

Today I am grateful for:

Week Ending: _____

⑦

My Week in Review

My top win this week was:

_____

_____

_____

I am grateful for:

_____

_____

_____

What could be improved or learned:

_____

_____

_____

Week Starting: _____ (8)

My Top 5 for this Week

Top 1 Done

○ ☐ _____

○ ☐ _____

○ ☐ _____

○ ☐ _____

○ ☐ _____

Are these aligned with my Monthly Top 5?

Progress > Perfection - Just Start

My top 5 for today

Top 1   Done

○ ☐ _____

○ ☐ _____

○ ☐ _____

○ ☐ _____

○ ☐ _____

Are these aligned with my Weekly Top 5?

Make progress your morning ritual—no excuses allowed.

Date: _____ Day: _____ (15)

My top win today was:

Today I am grateful for:

My top 5 for today

Top 1 Done

○ ☐ _____

○ ☐ _____

○ ☐ _____

○ ☐ _____

○ ☐ _____

Are these aligned with my Weekly Top 5?

Show the world you're serious—start making moves.

Date: _____ Day: _____ (16)

My top win today was: _____

Today I am grateful for: _____

My top 5 for today

Top 1 Done

○ ☐ _____

○ ☐ _____

○ ☐ _____

○ ☐ _____

○ ☐ _____

Are these aligned with my Weekly Top 5?

Believe in the magic that happens when you trust yourself.

Date: _____ Day: _____ (17)

My top win today was: _____

Today I am grateful for: _____

My top 5 for today

Top 1 Done

◯ ☐ _____

◯ ☐ _____

◯ ☐ _____

◯ ☐ _____

◯ ☐ _____

Are these aligned with my Weekly Top 5?

Give the day your all, and watch your goals come to life.

Date: _____ Day: _____ (18)

My top win today was:

Today I am grateful for:

My top 5 for today

Top 1   Done

○ ☐ _____

○ ☐ _____

○ ☐ _____

○ ☐ _____

○ ☐ _____

Are these aligned with my Weekly Top 5?

Show up with conviction—show the world you're serious.

Date: _____ Day: _____ (19)

My top win today was: _____

Today I am grateful for: _____

My top 5 for today

Top 1 Done

○ ☐ _____

○ ☐ _____

○ ☐ _____

○ ☐ _____

○ ☐ _____

Are these aligned with my Weekly Top 5?

Light up the present with your focus,
and future doors swing open.

Date: _____ Day: _____ 20

My top win today was: _____

Today I am grateful for: _____

My top 5 for today

Top 1   Done

○ ☐ _____

○ ☐ _____

○ ☐ _____

○ ☐ _____

○ ☐ _____

Are these aligned with my Weekly Top 5?

Hold tight to your priorities before
distractions get their hold on you.

Date: _____ Day: _____ (21)

My top win today was: _____

Today I am grateful for: _____

Week Ending: _____

My Week in Review

My top win this week was:

_____
_____
_____

I am grateful for:

_____
_____
_____

What could be improved or learned:

_____
_____
_____

Week Starting: _____

My Top 5 for this Week

Top 1 Done

○ ☐ _____

○ ☐ _____

○ ☐ _____

○ ☐ _____

○ ☐ _____

Are these aligned with my Monthly Top 5?

Progress beats perfection.
Take one step forward this week.

My top 5 for today

Top 1   Done

○ ☐ _____

○ ☐ _____

○ ☐ _____

○ ☐ _____

○ ☐ _____

Are these aligned with my Weekly Top 5?

Silence from others can echo your own voice louder—listen to it.

Date: _____ Day: _____ (22)

My top win today was: _____

Today I am grateful for: _____

My top 5 for today

Top 1 Done

○ ☐ _____

○ ☐ _____

○ ☐ _____

○ ☐ _____

○ ☐ _____

Are these aligned with my Weekly Top 5?

Lift yourself up, because relying on others might leave you stuck in the dirt.

Date: _____   Day: _____   (23)

My top win today was:

Today I am grateful for:

My top 5 for today

Top 1   Done

○ ☐ _____

○ ☐ _____

○ ☐ _____

○ ☐ _____

○ ☐ _____

Are these aligned with my Weekly Top 5?

Build structure today for success tomorrow.

Date: _____   Day: _____   (24)

My top win today was: _____

Today I am grateful for: _____

My top 5 for today

Top 1 Done
○ ☐ _____

○ ☐ _____

○ ☐ _____

○ ☐ _____

○ ☐ _____

Are these aligned with my Weekly Top 5?

Simplicity in your schedule lets you focus on what truly counts.

Date: _____ Day: _____ (25)

My top win today was:

Today I am grateful for:

My top 5 for today

Top 1   Done

○ ☐ _____

○ ☐ _____

○ ☐ _____

○ ☐ _____

○ ☐ _____

Are these aligned with my Weekly Top 5?

Celebrate yourself like you're your own best friend.

Date: _____ Day: _____ (26)

My top win today was: _____

Today I am grateful for: _____

My top 5 for today

Top 1 Done

○ ☐ _____

○ ☐ _____

○ ☐ _____

○ ☐ _____

○ ☐ _____

Are these aligned with my Weekly Top 5?

Act first, sort details later—action drives clarity.

Date: _____ Day: _____ (27)

My top win today was:

Today I am grateful for:

My top 5 for today

Top 1 Done

○ ☐ _____

○ ☐ _____

○ ☐ _____

○ ☐ _____

○ ☐ _____

Are these aligned with my Weekly Top 5?

Self-belief is the seed from which greatness grows.

Date: _____ Day: _____ (28)

My top win today was: _____

Today I am grateful for: _____

Week Ending: _____

My Week in Review

My top win this week was:

_____
_____

I am grateful for:

_____
_____

What could be improved or learned:

_____
_____

Week Starting: _____

(10)

My Top 5 for this Week

Top 1   Done

○ ☐ _____

○ ☐ _____

○ ☐ _____

○ ☐ _____

○ ☐ _____

Are these aligned with my Monthly Top 5?

Perfection is a thief. Progress is the real prize.

My top 5 for today

Top 1 Done

◯ ☐ _____

◯ ☐ _____

◯ ☐ _____

◯ ☐ _____

◯ ☐ _____

Are these aligned with my Weekly Top 5?

The best applause you'll ever receive is
the one you give yourself in triumph.

Date: _____ Day: _____ (29)

My top win today was:

Today I am grateful for:

My top 5 for today

Top 1   Done

○ ☐ _____

○ ☐ _____

○ ☐ _____

○ ☐ _____

○ ☐ _____

Are these aligned with my Weekly Top 5?

Let distractions fade so your priorities can shine brightly.

Date: _____ Day: _____ (30)

_____
_____
_____
_____
_____
_____
_____
_____
_____
_____
_____
_____
_____
_____
_____
_____
_____
_____
_____
_____
_____
_____
_____
_____

My top win today was: _____

Today I am grateful for: _____

My top 5 for today

Top 1   Done

○ □ _____

○ □ _____

○ □ _____

○ □ _____

○ □ _____

Are these aligned with my Weekly Top 5?

Simplicity is about focusing on the critical and ignoring the trivial

Date: _____ Day: _____ (31)

My top win today was: _____

Today I am grateful for: _____

Month: _____

My Month in Review

My top win last month was:

I am grateful for:

What could be improved or learned:

Month: _____

My Top 5 for this Month

Top 1 Done
○ ☐ _____

○ ☐ _____

○ ☐ _____

○ ☐ _____

○ ☐ _____

Are these aligned with my Quarterly Top 5?

Chasing perfection steals your time—
progress pays the real rewards.

Week Ending: _____ (10)

My Week in Review

My top win this week was:

_____
_____

I am grateful for:

_____
_____

What could be improved or learned:

_____
_____

Week Starting: _____

My Top 5 for this Week

Top 1 Done

○ ☐ _____

○ ☐ _____

○ ☐ _____

○ ☐ _____

○ ☐ _____

Are these aligned with my Monthly Top 5?

Perfection steals momentum. Progress builds success.

My top 5 for today

Top 1 Done

○ ☐ _____

○ ☐ _____

○ ☐ _____

○ ☐ _____

○ ☐ _____

Are these aligned with my Weekly Top 5?

Be your own alarm clock—wake yourself to unstoppable drive.

Date: _____ Day: _____ (1)

My top win today was: _____

Today I am grateful for: _____

My top 5 for today

Top 1   Done

○ ☐ _____

○ ☐ _____

○ ☐ _____

○ ☐ _____

○ ☐ _____

Are these aligned with my Weekly Top 5?

Leave the ideal behind; the real journey is about progress.

Date: _____ Day: _____   (2)

My top win today was: _____

Today I am grateful for: _____

My top 5 for today

Top 1   Done
○ ☐ _____

○ ☐ _____

○ ☐ _____

○ ☐ _____

○ ☐ _____

Are these aligned with my Weekly Top 5?

Reserve space in your day for what
genuinely lights you up.

Date: _____   Day: _____   (3)

My top win today was:

Today I am grateful for:

My top 5 for today

Top 1 Done

◯ ☐ _____

◯ ☐ _____

◯ ☐ _____

◯ ☐ _____

◯ ☐ _____

Are these aligned with my Weekly Top 5?

Be unafraid of your unique journey—it
leads to your truest self.

Date: _____   Day: _____   (4)

My top win today was: _____

Today I am grateful for: _____

My top 5 for today

Top 1 Done

○ ☐ _____

○ ☐ _____

○ ☐ _____

○ ☐ _____

○ ☐ _____

Are these aligned with my Weekly Top 5?

Your effort sparks the engine of progress.

Date: _____ Day: _____ (5)

My top win today was: _____

Today I am grateful for: _____

My top 5 for today

Top 1 Done

○ ☐ _____

○ ☐ _____

○ ☐ _____

○ ☐ _____

○ ☐ _____

Are these aligned with my Weekly Top 5?

Remember that your path is yours alone,
so tread it boldly.

Date: _____ Day: _____ (6)

My top win today was:

Today I am grateful for:

My top 5 for today

Top 1 Done

○ ☐ _____

○ ☐ _____

○ ☐ _____

○ ☐ _____

○ ☐ _____

Are these aligned with my Weekly Top 5?

Thankfulness is a gentle wind propelling you toward your brightest future.

Date: _____ Day: _____   (7)

My top win today was:

Today I am grateful for:

Week Ending: _____

My Week in Review

My top win this week was:

_____
_____
_____

I am grateful for:

_____
_____
_____

What could be improved or learned:

_____
_____
_____

Week Starting: _____

My Top 5 for this Week

Top 1 Done

○ ☐ _____

○ ☐ _____

○ ☐ _____

○ ☐ _____

○ ☐ _____

Are these aligned with my Monthly Top 5?

Own the week—start strong, finish stronger.

My top 5 for today

Top 1   Done

○ ☐ _____

○ ☐ _____

○ ☐ _____

○ ☐ _____

○ ☐ _____

Are these aligned with my Weekly Top 5?

Kickstart your hustle; fortune favours the proactive.

Date: _____ Day: _____ (8)

My top win today was:

Today I am grateful for:

My top 5 for today

Top 1   Done

○ ☐ _____

○ ☐ _____

○ ☐ _____

○ ☐ _____

○ ☐ _____

Are these aligned with my Weekly Top 5?

Productivity is fuelled by clarity—know what matters most.

Date: _____ Day: _____ (9)

My top win today was: _____

Today I am grateful for: _____

My top 5 for today

Top 1 Done

○ ☐ _____

○ ☐ _____

○ ☐ _____

○ ☐ _____

○ ☐ _____

Are these aligned with my Weekly Top 5?

Busy is often loud; real productivity speaks for itself.

Date: _____ Day: _____ (10)

My top win today was:

Today I am grateful for:

My top 5 for today

Top 1 Done
○ ☐ _____

○ ☐ _____

○ ☐ _____

○ ☐ _____

○ ☐ _____

Are these aligned with my Weekly Top 5?

Kickstart your hustle—your future is waiting.

Date: _____ Day: _____   (11)

My top win today was: _____

Today I am grateful for: _____

My top 5 for today

Top 1   Done

○ □ _____

○ □ _____

○ □ _____

○ □ _____

○ □ _____

Are these aligned with my Weekly Top 5?

Productivity is the art of turning ideas into accomplishments.

Date: _____ Day: _____   (12)

My top win today was: _____

Today I am grateful for: _____

My top 5 for today

Top 1   Done

◯ ☐ _____

◯ ☐ _____

◯ ☐ _____

◯ ☐ _____

◯ ☐ _____

Are these aligned with my Weekly Top 5?

The greatest gift to your future self is
your wholehearted presence now.

Date: _____   Day: _____   (13)

My top win today was:

Today I am grateful for:

My top 5 for today

Top 1 Done

○ ☐ _____

○ ☐ _____

○ ☐ _____

○ ☐ _____

○ ☐ _____

Are these aligned with my Weekly Top 5?

Your future self thanks you for grinding today.

Date: _____ Day: _____ (14)

My top win today was: _____

Today I am grateful for: _____

Week Ending: _____

My Week in Review

My top win this week was:

_____
_____
_____

I am grateful for:

_____
_____
_____

What could be improved or learned:

_____
_____

Week Starting: _____

My Top 5 for this Week

Top 1 Done

○ ☐ _____

○ ☐ _____

○ ☐ _____

○ ☐ _____

○ ☐ _____

Are these aligned with my Monthly Top 5?

Every day is a step forward—stack them wisely.

My top 5 for today

Top 1 Done

○ ☐ _____

○ ☐ _____

○ ☐ _____

○ ☐ _____

○ ☐ _____

Are these aligned with my Weekly Top 5?

Productivity thrives when excuses die.

Date: _____ Day: _____ (15)

My top win today was:

Today I am grateful for:

My top 5 for today

Top 1 Done

○ ☐ _____

○ ☐ _____

○ ☐ _____

○ ☐ _____

○ ☐ _____

Are these aligned with my Weekly Top 5?

The greatest gift you can give yourself is permission to be you.

Date: _____ Day: _____ (16)

My top win today was: _____

Today I am grateful for: _____

My top 5 for today

Top 1   Done
◯ ☐ _____

◯ ☐ _____

◯ ☐ _____

◯ ☐ _____

◯ ☐ _____

Are these aligned with my Weekly Top 5?

Your future thrives on action, not on perfection.

Date: _____ Day: _____ (17)

My top win today was: _____

Today I am grateful for: _____

My top 5 for today

Top 1 Done

○ ☐ _____

○ ☐ _____

○ ☐ _____

○ ☐ _____

○ ☐ _____

Are these aligned with my Weekly Top 5?

Purposeful planning is useless without purposeful doing.

Date: _____ Day: _____ (18)

My top win today was: _____

Today I am grateful for: _____

My top 5 for today

Top 1 Done

○ ☐ _____

○ ☐ _____

○ ☐ _____

○ ☐ _____

○ ☐ _____

Are these aligned with my Weekly Top 5?

Don't base your worth on how they treat you—make self-respect non-negotiable.

Date: _____ Day: _____ (19)

My top win today was: _____

Today I am grateful for: _____

My top 5 for today

Top 1 Done
○ ☐ _____

○ ☐ _____

○ ☐ _____

○ ☐ _____

○ ☐ _____

Are these aligned with my Weekly Top 5?

Your goals deserve more action than excuses.

Date: _____ Day: _____ (20)

My top win today was: _____

Today I am grateful for: _____

My top 5 for today

Top 1 Done

○ ☐ _____

○ ☐ _____

○ ☐ _____

○ ☐ _____

○ ☐ _____

Are these aligned with my Weekly Top 5?

Pursue better daily, and best becomes inevitable.

Date: _____ Day: _____ (21)

My top win today was: _____

Today I am grateful for: _____

Week Ending: _____

My Week in Review

My top win this week was:
_____
_____
_____

I am grateful for:
_____
_____
_____

What could be improved or learned:
_____
_____
_____

Week Starting: _____   (14)

My Top 5 for this Week

Top 1 Done

○ ☐ _____

○ ☐ _____

○ ☐ _____

○ ☐ _____

○ ☐ _____

Are these aligned with my Monthly Top 5?

Win the morning, win the week.

My top 5 for today

Top 1　Done

○ ☐ _____

○ ☐ _____

○ ☐ _____

○ ☐ _____

○ ☐ _____

Are these aligned with my Weekly Top 5?

The more often you pause to say thanks,
the more reasons you find to smile.

Date: _____ Day: _____ (22)

My top win today was: _____

Today I am grateful for: _____

My top 5 for today

Top 1   Done

○ ☐ _____

○ ☐ _____

○ ☐ _____

○ ☐ _____

○ ☐ _____

Are these aligned with my Weekly Top 5?

Your hustle today becomes tomorrow's reward.

Date: _____ Day: _____ (23)

My top win today was: _____

Today I am grateful for: _____

My top 5 for today

Top 1 Done
○ ☐ _____

○ ☐ _____

○ ☐ _____

○ ☐ _____

○ ☐ _____

Are these aligned with my Weekly Top 5?

Put your vision into motion—only you can ignite the spark.

Date: _____ Day: _____ (24)

_____
_____
_____
_____
_____
_____
_____
_____
_____
_____
_____
_____
_____
_____
_____
_____
_____
_____
_____
_____
_____
_____
_____
_____
_____

My top win today was: _____
_____

Today I am grateful for: _____

My top 5 for today

Top 1   Done

○ ☐ _____

○ ☐ _____

○ ☐ _____

○ ☐ _____

○ ☐ _____

Are these aligned with my Weekly Top 5?

You can't fail at being yourself—embrace your true nature.

Date: _____ Day: _____ (25)

My top win today was: _____

Today I am grateful for: _____

My top 5 for today

Top 1 Done

○ ☐ _____

○ ☐ _____

○ ☐ _____

○ ☐ _____

○ ☐ _____
Are these aligned with my Weekly Top 5?

Your legacy is written by your progress,
not by a perfect plan.

Date: _____ Day: _____ (26)

My top win today was: _____

Today I am grateful for: _____

My top 5 for today

Top 1   Done

○ ☐ _____

○ ☐ _____

○ ☐ _____

○ ☐ _____

○ ☐ _____

Are these aligned with my Weekly Top 5?

Quiet the noise of doubt; your heart holds the answers.

Date: _____ Day: _____ (27)

My top win today was: _____

Today I am grateful for: _____

My top 5 for today

Top 1 Done

○ ☐ ....

○ ☐ ....

○ ☐ ....

○ ☐ ....

○ ☐ ....

Are these aligned with my Weekly Top 5?

Discipline is destiny—hone it, and you shape your future.

Date: _____ Day: _____ (28)

My top win today was: _____

Today I am grateful for: _____

Week Ending: _____

My Week in Review

My top win this week was:

_____
_____
_____

I am grateful for:

_____
_____
_____

What could be improved or learned:

_____
_____

Week Starting: _____

My Top 5 for this Week

Top 1 Done

○ ☐ _____

○ ☐ _____

○ ☐ _____

○ ☐ _____

○ ☐ _____

Are these aligned with my Monthly Top 5?

A productive week starts with a single focused task.

My top 5 for today

Top 1 Done

○ ☐ _____

○ ☐ _____

○ ☐ _____

○ ☐ _____

○ ☐ _____

Are these aligned with my Weekly Top 5?

Keep going—time rewards consistent effort.

Date: _____ Day: _____ (29)

My top win today was: _____

Today I am grateful for: _____

My top 5 for today

Top 1 Done

○ ☐ _____

○ ☐ _____

○ ☐ _____

○ ☐ _____

○ ☐ _____

Are these aligned with my Weekly Top 5?

Race against your own limits, not the ticking clock.

Date: _____ Day: _____ (30)

_____

My top win today was: _____

Today I am grateful for: _____

My top 5 for today

Top 1   Done

○ ☐ _____

○ ☐ _____

○ ☐ _____

○ ☐ _____

○ ☐ _____

Are these aligned with my Weekly Top 5?

They might not be proud of you—be proud
of yourself for continuing anyway.

Date: _____ Day: _____ (31)

My top win today was:

Today I am grateful for:

Quarter: _____ to _____

My 3 Big Priorities This Quarter

Priority 1:

_____

_____

Priority 2:

_____

_____

Priority 3:

_____

_____

How Did I Go on My Big 3?

Priority 1:

_____

_____

Priority 2:

_____

_____

Priority 3:

_____

_____

Notes

Perfection is a thief.

SAM PENNY
The Topify Method

topifymethod.com

www.ingramcontent.com/pod-product-compliance
Lightning Source LLC
Chambersburg PA
CBHW072150200426
43209CB00052B/1104